Let's DRAW!

DRAGONS

How2DrawAnimals

Brimming with creative inspiration, how-to projects, and useful information to enrich your everyday life, quarto.com is a favorite destination for those pursuing their interests and passions.

© 2022 Quarto Publishing Group USA Inc.
Illustrations and text © 2022 P. Mendoza

First published in 2022 by Walter Foster Jr., an imprint of The Quarto Group.
100 Cummings Center, Suite 265D, Beverly, MA 01915, USA.
T (978) 282-9590 F (978) 283-2742 www.quarto.com • www.walterfoster.com

Walter Foster Jr. titles are also available at discount for retail, wholesale, promotional, and bulk purchase. For details, contact the Special Sales Manager by email at specialsales@quarto.com or by mail at The Quarto Group, Attn: Special Sales Manager, 100 Cummings Center, Suite 265D, Beverly, MA 01915, USA.

ISBN: 978-0-7603-8084-0

Digital edition published in 2022
eISBN: 978-0-7603-8085-7

Printed in China
10 9 8 7 6 5 4

TABLE OF CONTENTS

TOOLS & MATERIALS

Welcome! You don't need much to start learning how to draw. Anyone can draw with just a pencil and piece of scrap paper, but if you want to get more serious about your art, additional artist's supplies are available.

PAPER If you choose printer paper, buy a premium paper that is thick enough and bright. Portable sketch pads keep all your drawings in one place, which is convenient. For more detailed art pieces, use a fine art paper.

PENCILS Standard No. 2 pencils and mechanical pencils are great to start with and inexpensive. Pencils with different graphite grades can be very helpful when shading because a specific grade (such as 4H, 2B, or HB) will only get so dark.

PENCIL SHARPENER Electric sharpeners are faster than manual ones, but they also wear down pencils faster. It's most economical to use an automatic one for inexpensive pencils and a manual sharpener for expensive ones.

ERASERS Some erasers can smear, bend, and even tear your paper, so get a good one that erases cleanly without smudges. Kneaded erasers are pliable and can be molded for precise erasing. They leave no residue, and they last a long time.

PENS If you want to outline a drawing after sketching it, you can use a regular Sharpie® pen or marker. For more intricate pieces, try Micron® pens, which come in a variety of tip thicknesses.

DRAWING BASICS

How to Draw Shapes

For the first steps of each project in this book, you will be drawing basic shapes as guide lines. Use light, smooth strokes and don't press down too hard with your pencil. If you sketch lightly at first, it will be easier to erase if you make a mistake.

You'll be drawing a lot of circles, which many beginning artists find difficult to create. These circles do not have to be perfect because they are just guides, but if you want to practice making better circles, try the four-marks method, as shown below.

1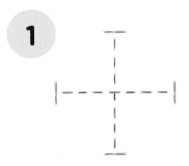

Mark where you want the top of the circle and, directly below, make another mark for the bottom. Do the same for the sides of the circle. If it helps, lightly draw a dotted line to help you place the other mark.

2

Once you have the four marks spaced apart equally, connect them using curved lines.

3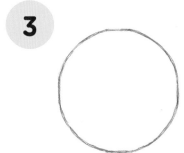

Erase any dotted lines you created, and you have a circle!

ADDITIONAL SHAPES While circles are usually what people find the most challenging, there are many other lines and shapes that you should practice and master. An arc can become a muzzle or tongue. Triangles can be ears, teeth, or claws. A football shape can become an eye. A curvy line can make a tail and an angled line a leg. Study the animal and note the shapes that stand out to you.

How to Shade

The final step to drawing an animal is to add shading so that it looks three-dimensional, and then adding texture so that it looks furry, feathery, smooth, or scaly. To introduce yourself to shading, follow the steps below.

1

Understand your pencil with a value scale. Using any pencil, start to shade lightly on one side and gradually darken your strokes toward the other side. This value scale will show you how light and dark your pencil can be.

2

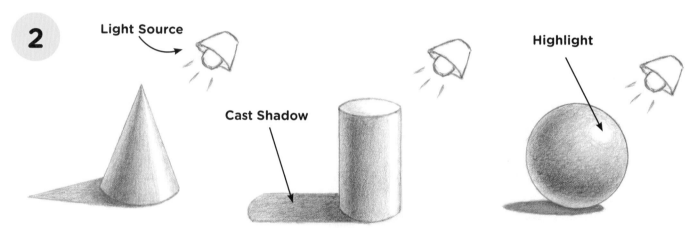

Light Source

Cast Shadow

Highlight

Apply the value scale to simple shapes. Draw simple shapes and shade them to make them look three-dimensional. Observe shadows in real life. Study how the light interacts with simple objects and creates shadows. Then try drawing what you see.

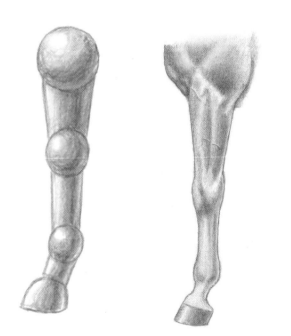

3

Practice with more complex objects. Once you're comfortable shading simple objects, move on to more complex ones. Note, for example, how a horse's leg is made up of cylinders and spheres. Breaking down your subject into simple shapes makes it easier to visualize the shadows.

How to Add Texture

Take what you've learned about shading one step further by adding texture to your drawings.

FURRY

One quick pencil stroke creates a single hair. Keep adding more quick, short strokes and you'll get a furry texture. Separate each individual stroke a bit so that the white of the paper comes through.

Create stripes and patterns by varying the pressure on your pencil to get different degrees of tonal value.

Make sure that your strokes follow the forms of the animal. As you shade a furry animal, use strokes that go in the general direction of the fur growth. The fur here follows the form of a simple sphere.

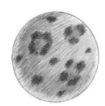

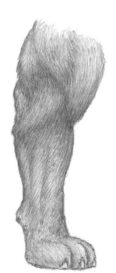

This is how to add fur to a complex form, which is easier if you know the animal's anatomy. In order to show the muscle structure, this image shows an exaggerated example of a lion's front leg and paw.

SMOOTH

For very short fur or smooth skin, add graphite evenly. Blend with a cotton swab, blending stump, or piece of tissue if needed.

SCALY

For scaly animals like reptiles or dragons, create each individual scale with a tiny arc. Then add shadows to make the form look three-dimensional.

For a much easier way to get a scaly look, just add a bunch of squiggles! Make the squiggles darker in areas of pattern, as well as when adding shadows.

FEATHERED When adding texture to feathered animals, approach it as you would with fur or with smooth skin. Use a series of short strokes for fine or fluffy feathers. For smooth feathers, use even, blended value.

MEDIEVAL DRAGON

Begin by lightly sketching three circles. These guides will help you create the head and body, so pay attention to the size and placement of each shape. These guides are important because they establish the body proportions of your dragon.

Draw an arc next to the head as a guide for the muzzle. Connect the body shapes with curved lines, and for the tail, draw a couple of lines that meet at a point on the left side.

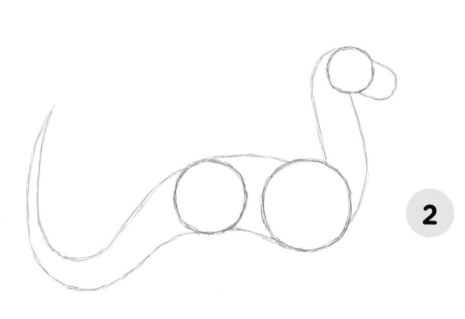

Add angled lines below the body as guides for the legs, and draw an angled line on top of the body for the wings. Make sure you are happy with the proportions before moving on to the next step.

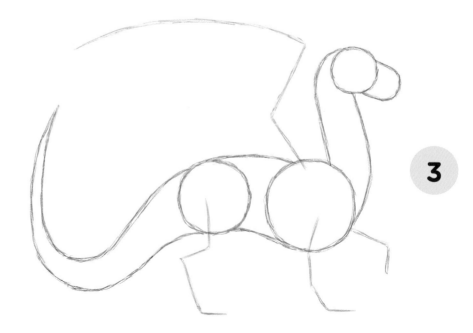

4

Draw the eye and add some lines surrounding it for extra detail. Draw jagged lines above for a bony brow and complete the top part of the mouth, including the triangular teeth.

EYES Your eyes might end up too small to add a lot of detail. If you draw the head large enough for detailed eyes, make sure include a tiny circle off to the side for a highlight. In the middle of the eye, draw a slightly bigger circle for the pupil and shade it with a dark value. When you shade the rest of the eye, don't overlap the small highlight circle.

Use wavy lines to draw the lower part of the mouth. Include tiny triangles to create the sharp teeth.

5

6

Complete the head by adding a spike on the chin, the nostril, two horns, and a fin-like ear.

To draw the first wing, thicken up the guide line, especially at the base, and draw a pointy spike on the top. Add some curved lines to show the bony structure, and then use more curved lines for the skin that connects them.

7

Sketch the first two legs using curved lines to emphasize the muscles. Add a big spike on the back of the large hind leg, and draw a couple of toes and nails on each foot.

8

Draw the visible portion of the hind leg on the other side and then add the lifted front leg. Draw the visible part of the wing on the other side using the first wing as a guide.

9

Draw the neck and body using the initial shapes and lines as guides. Use small lines on the right side of the neck to represent scales and add spikes on the back and down the tail. Draw a large arrow-like shape at the end for extra detail.

10

For a cleaner look, erase as much as you can of the initial guide lines. Don't worry about erasing all of them. It's okay to leave some behind. Also re-draw any final sketch lines that you may have accidentally erased.

11

First add some shadows on and underneath your dragon's body to make it look more three-dimensional. To get this rough, scaly look, draw squiggles all over the body. Press harder in the areas where there are stripes. Dragons are mythical creatures, so be creative and draw yours any way you'd like!

12

SLEEPING DRAGON

Lightly sketch a circle and a long arc for the head guide.

1

With basic shapes, draw guides for the tucked-under legs. Then draw a big arc over these shapes for the body.

2

On top of the body, draw a big, triangular shape as the guide for the wings. For the tail, draw wavy lines that come to a point near the dragon's head.

3

Draw the closed eye and add three small, spiky shapes for the bony brow. Add a few more small lines around the eye for detail.

4

Darken the initial arc for the muzzle. Add a small bump on the top for the nostril and a curve at the bottom, right for the jaw. Create the mouth with a wavy line and add teeth. Draw the second nostril and add three spikes for the brow on the other side of the head.

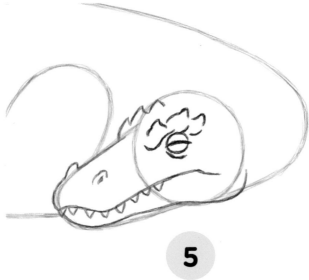

5

Starting between the two brow ridges, draw a series of small, triangular shapes for the spikes on the neck. Then add the pointy horns without overlapping the spikes. Draw three on this side of the head and the two visible ones on the other side.

6

Use the shape to the left of the head as a guide to draw the front leg, making sure not to overlap what you drew for the head. Curve the lines for muscle definition and add a spike on the elbow.

7

Draw the folded hind leg, including the spike, toes, and claws. Don't overlap the front leg. Part of the claws will be hidden behind it.

8

Create the first folded wing. On the right, draw a spike on the joint, and on the left, draw three long, triangular shapes to create the bottom part of the wing. Finally, draw the part of the wing that attaches to the body.

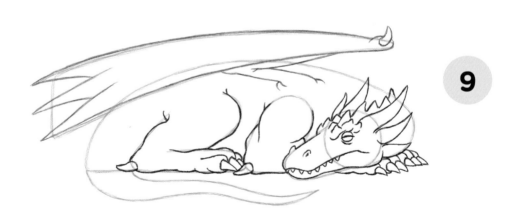

9

Darken the neck without overlapping the horns, and draw the tail. Draw spikes along the neck and tail, and add an arrow-like shape at the tip of the tail. Finally, draw what's visible of the other wing using the first wing as a template.

10

Finalize your lines in this step by erasing any lines you don't want to keep and re-drawing lines you do want.

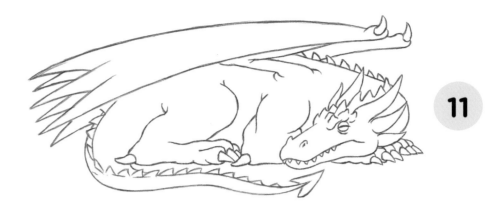

11

12

Add some shadows to your drawing, including a little bit of a cast shadow underneath. Use a medium value on most of the body and very light value on the underside. The horns, spikes, and claws are a very dark value. Add value lightly at first and gradually build up to the level of darkness that you like.

DIMENSION & VOLUME To make a two-dimensional drawing look three-dimensional, decide where the light source should be, and create shadows where they would appear in real life (if dragons were real!). To get light and dark values, vary the pressure on your pencil. Be sure to shade lightly at first, and then gradually build up to the level of darkness that you like. Adding accurate shadows to drawings takes time and practice to do well, so for now, observe your references (in this case, the final step) and copy what you see, taking note where the shadows are.

WYVERN

1

Lightly sketch two circles. The farther apart these two circles are, the longer the wyvern's neck will be. Draw an arc on the bottom of the larger circle, which will be the lower half of the body.

2

Add two curved lines inside the head as guide lines to place the facial features later on. Draw a small arc as a guide for the muzzle, connect the head and body to form the neck, and add basic shapes at the bottom to create legs and feet.

3

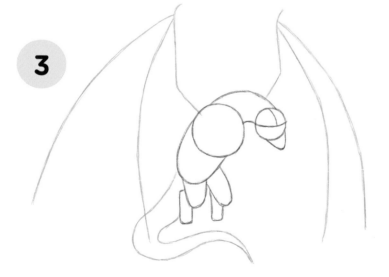

Add the tail at the bottom as two lines that come to a point at the tip. Then draw the wing guides. Draw two angled lines up from the body and neck guides. Then, starting near the top of each line, draw two long, curved lines down toward the feet.

4

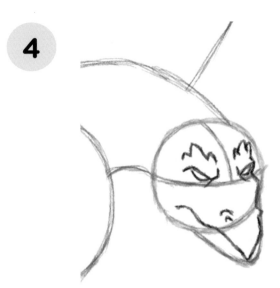

Draw the eyes with a few angled lines. For a menacing look, don't include irises or pupils. Add the bony brows above with curved lines and draw the pointy muzzle. Don't forget the nostrils.

5

Finish the mouth and add a downward-pointing horn on the lower jaw. Draw three more spikes on this side of the head and the two on the other side that are visible from this angle.

6

Draw the first part of the wing. Follow the path of the vertical guide and draw the thin arm-like shape around it. Then draw the triangle-like portion with three V shapes at the bottom for the folded edge of the wing.

7

Draw the wing on the other side the same way, but add two V shapes at the bottom instead of three.

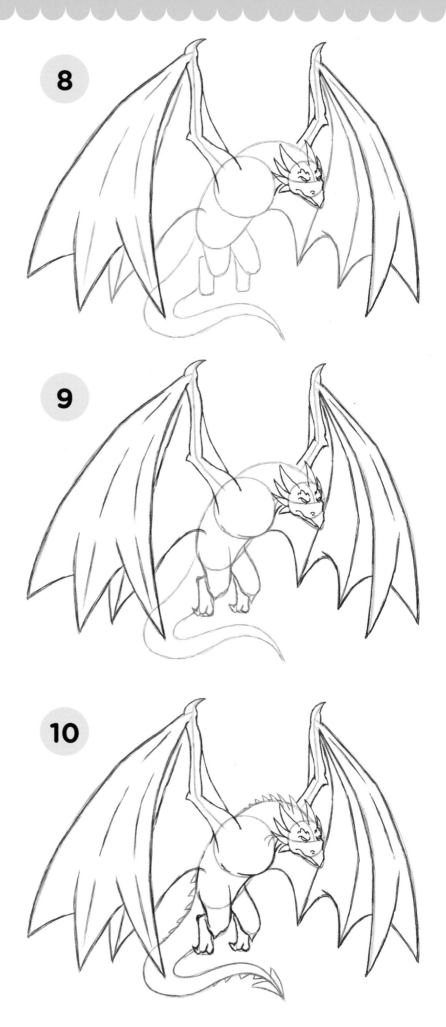

8

Complete the wings with additional lines and V shapes at the bottom. Connect the bottom parts of the wings to the body guide.

9

Use the shapes under the neck to create the body, and then draw the legs and feet. Add a spike at the joint and draw the toes pointing backward.

10

Draw the neck and tail, including spikes and an arrow-like shape at the tip of the tail. As you draw the tail, make sure not to overlap the wing tip.

11

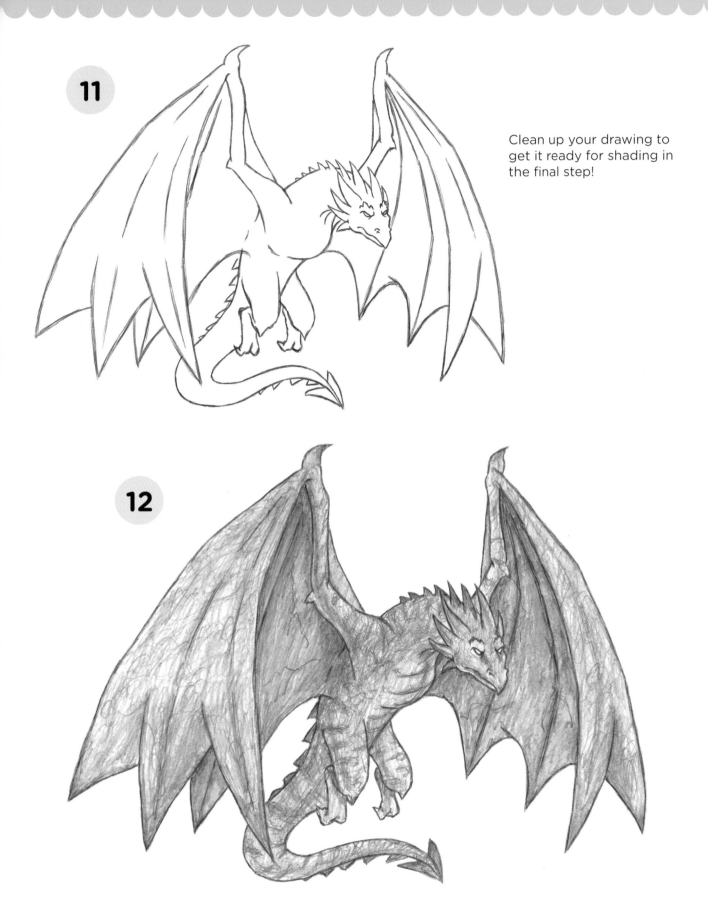

Clean up your drawing to get it ready for shading in the final step!

12

Add some shading to your wyvern, using a dark value for the shadows to give the figure more dimension and volume. Shade the rest of the body with a medium value. Don't worry about shading too smoothly; the rough value gives the skin texture. Add some lines to the wings for veins, make the spikes darker, and draw a few lines on the chest for scales. For a rough texture and an almost granite-like look, add squiggly lines all over the body.

FIRE DRAGON

1

First draw two circles. Note their size and placement in relation to each other. Add two lines within the smaller head circle to help you place the facial features. Finally, add the neck as two curved lines that connect the head to the body circle.

2

Draw two angled lines at the top as guides for the wings. Two arcs coming off of the head circle will create the mouth, and some basic shapes below the body will become the front legs.

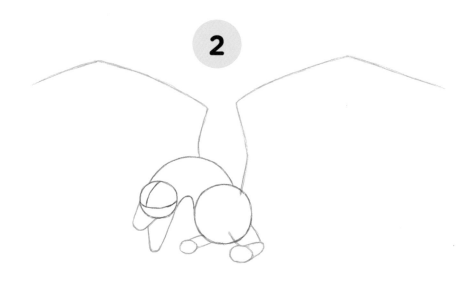

3

Because of the perspective, the back half of the body looks smaller because it is receding in the distance. A pointy arc makes the back part of the body. From there, create the tail guide with two wavy lines that come to a point. Several shapes make up the back foot.

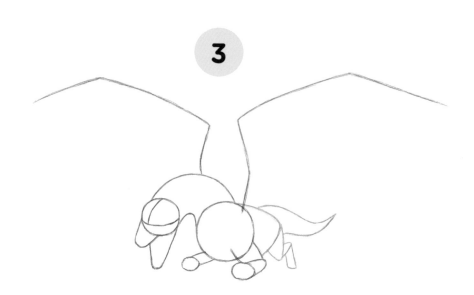

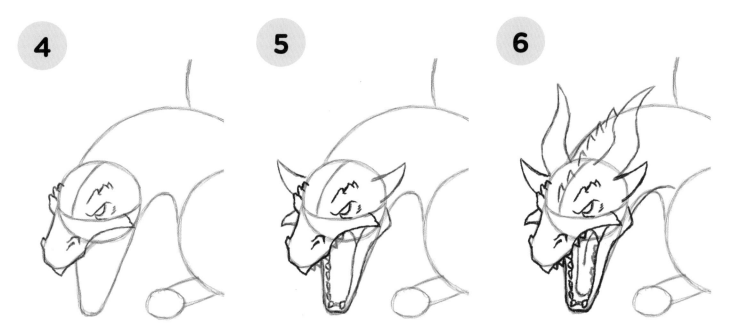

4

For a fierce look, add the eyes without irises or pupils. Pay close attention to all of the lines around the eye. Add the spiky brows and complete the pointy muzzle. Don't forget the nostrils.

5

Draw the mouth and jaw, and add some teeth. Don't forget the small line on the top-right of the mouth for the piece of skin that connects the jaws. Add the other jaw spike and two horns on the head.

6

Complete the mouth by adding the tongue and the rest of the teeth. Add two larger horns on the head, a series of short spikes in the middle, and part of the neck.

7

Draw more spikes on the long neck. Because of the perspective, the spikes should get smaller farther down the neck. Create the shape of the dragon's chest, and then draw the first front leg.

8

Draw the other front leg the same way as the first. For the hind leg, simply darken the outer edges of the initial guides. Then add a couple of short lines that curve to the right for the toes and claws.

9

Follow the path of each wing guide as you make the shape thicker. Leave a gap on the inside where the shape bends and add a small spike above that. Darken the shape of the tail and add a few spikes along the top.

10

On either side, draw two more long, bony shapes originating from the gap you left in the last step. Connect the tips with curved lines to represent the skin that connects the bony structures. Make sure to connect the wings to the body.

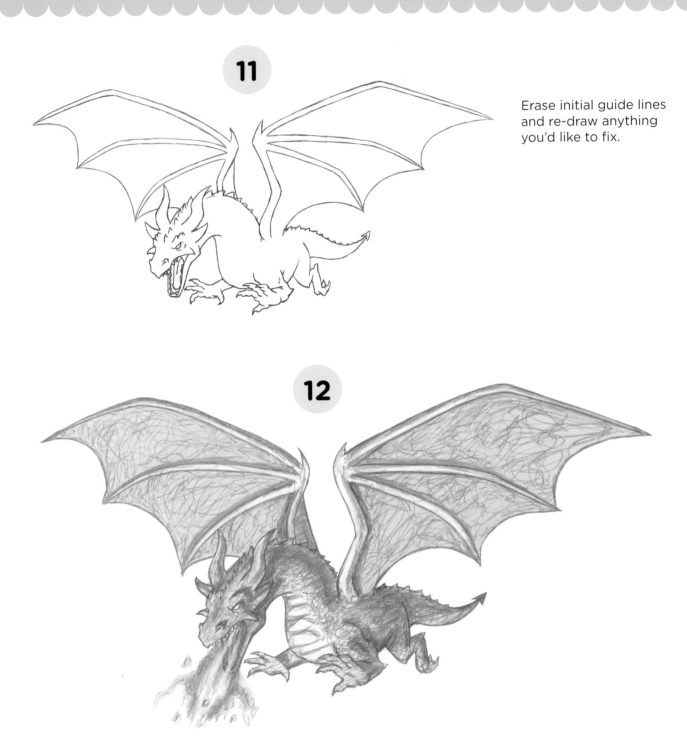

11

Erase initial guide lines and re-draw anything you'd like to fix.

12

Add some shading to give your dragon more dimension and volume. Because flames will be coming from the mouth, the shadows will mainly be on the right, away from the mouth. Create horizontal lines on the chest. Then use tiny, squiggly lines all over the body to represent the skin's rough, scaly texture. Lastly, create the fiery breath.

FIERY BREATH To make a dragon look like it's breathing fire, first draw an open mouth. Lightly erase a bit of the mouth, and then draw a few thick columns with a smooth medium value and a diagonal orientation. Add more value at the bottom for smoke and small shapes for debris.

ICE DRAGON

Lightly sketch three circles as guides for the head and body. Pay attention to the sizes and placement of these circles because they are important for establishing the proportions of the dragon.

Draw a small arc on the head circle as a guide for the muzzle. Connect the head and body shapes with curved lines, and then create a tail on the left.

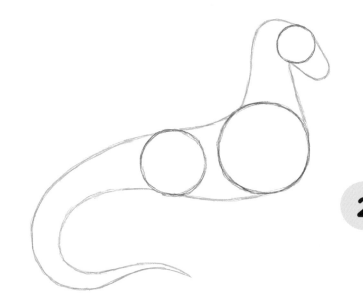

Add four angled lines below the body as guides for the legs. Bend the guides where the joints will be. The wing is made up of four slightly curved lines of different lengths and orientations.

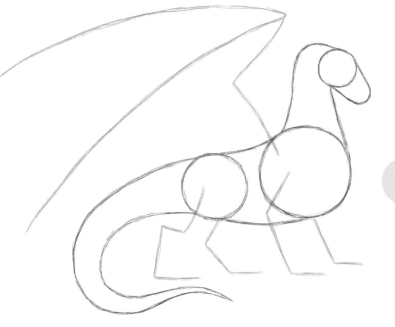

4

Draw a fierce-looking eye with a couple of angled lines. Draw the thick, spiky brows and the muzzle, including spikes for the nostrils and a spike on the chin. For the mouth and teeth, draw a series of spiky shapes.

5

Create three spikes on top of the head starting in between the brow ridges. Then add a much larger horn on either side of the head. Complete the head horns with three triangular spikes on the jaw.

6

Draw the thick base of the wing and add a spike at the two joints. Darken the long, curved lines on the left and draw spikes at the ends. Add a third spike in between, and then connect the spikes with curved lines to form the edge of the wing.

Draw the first two legs using curved lines to emphasize the muscle structure. Add sharp claws on the toes and a small, diamond-like shape on the back of the front leg.

7

Using the first legs as a template, draw what's visible of the two legs on the other side of the body. Then go back to the wing and add the underside with some curved lines and another spike. Complete the wing with some lines inside for structure. Then add the tip of the other wing.

8

Draw the plates of armor on the neck, chest, and underside of the body. There is one triangular plate near the shoulder, but the rest are rectangular or square-like.

9

Darken the rest of the neck and body, and add a series of small, triangle-like shapes for spikes. They are larger on the neck and get smaller down the back and tail. At the tip of the tail, draw an arrow-like spike.

10

Stop here for a sketch, or tidy up your sketch and move on to the final step to add shading to your drawing. Note how some of these thin, sleek shapes resemble icicles. These shapes are what help make this an ice dragon.

CAST SHADOWS
If your dragon isn't flying or swimming in your drawing, add a cast shadow underneath it. This will help ground the creature so it doesn't appear to be floating in space. Use a darker value near the middle of the shadow and a lighter value along the edge.

11

12

Add shadows throughout the body and on the ground underneath it. Then add a dark value to the body and top of the wings, and a medium value on the underside of the wings and sides of the chest plates. Leave the eyes, horns, spikes, claws, and shine on the chest plates white or use a very light value.

EARTH DRAGON

Begin with three circles.

1

Connect the circles and add a muzzle and tail.

2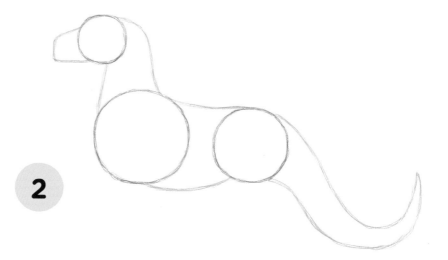

Add guides for the feet and large wing.

3

4

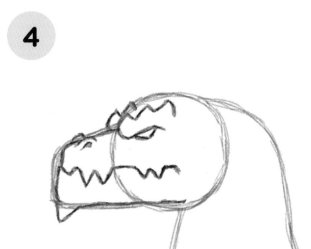

Draw the face using lots of angled lines to show the fierce eye, bony brow ridges, sharp teeth, and chin spike. The muzzle is square, and two nostrils protrude at the top. The thick, bold shapes on this dragon are reminiscent of rocks and tree trunks. These shapes help make this an earth dragon.

5

Three thick spikes come off the jaw and point in different directions. On top of the head, draw two sets of three horns that get gradually taller the farther back they go. The horns on the other side of the head are partially hidden.

6

Make the wing guide thicker as you follow the path of the guide line. Add a spike at the top, and connect the tip to the body using three curved lines.

Draw the two legs on this side of the body. Follow the path of the guides using curved lines to represent the muscle structure. Note how the hind leg will overlap the guide for the other hind leg. Draw three toes on each foot and add a triangular claw to the tip of each toe.

Using the wing and legs on this side of the body as templates, draw the limbs on the other side the same way. Only draw what's visible from this angle.

Use the remaining guides to draw the rest of the body. Don't overlap the shape of the wing or the legs on this side of the body, and don't close off the tip of the tail. Add a line along the neck and underside of the body to create the first part of the scales.

Complete the details of this dragon with triangular spikes along the back, protective scales on the underside, and a big club at the end of the tail.

10

Tidy up your drawing by erasing the initial guide lines.

11

Add shadows throughout the body and underneath it to give the form more dimension and volume. The darkest values will be in the shadowed areas, but use a dark value for the top of the body and wings, and a lighter value for the skin on the wings and underside of the body. Leave a bit on each claw blank.

12

WATER DRAGON

Start your initial sketch with three light circles that will make up the head and body.

1

Connect the head and body shapes, and add an open mouth and a long, thick tail.

2

Add the leg guides with shapes this time, rather than simpler angled lines. This will help you with the perspective. This dragon is floating in the water, and each limb will be viewed from a different angle. Because this is a water dragon, it has no wings.

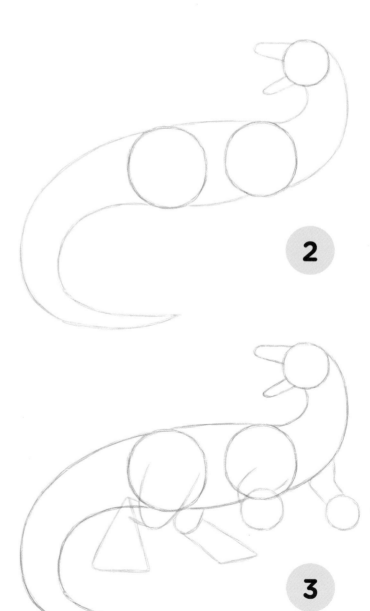

3

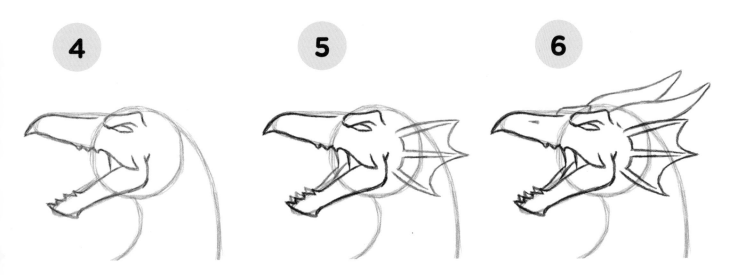

4

Add the diamond-shaped eye, eyebrow, and brow ridge. Then draw the thin, pointy muzzle. The mouth is open, so add some teeth and details where the jaws meet.

5

Complete the other side of the bottom jaw and add the fin-like ear.

6

Finish up the head with the nostril, the other brow ridge, and two backward-facing horns. The bottom edge of the horn will be hidden behind the ear.

7

Draw the two limbs that are on this side of the body by following the guides. Add the pointy webbed digits and a couple more small lines on the limbs for detail.

Draw the other two limbs the same way, including some small detail lines.

8

Use the remaining initial lines and shapes as guides to draw the rest of the body, leaving a gap on the tail where spikes will be. Draw a shark-like fin at the tip of the tail. Then add a few extra lines under the head and along the bottom of the body to create the underside.

9

Draw spikes down the back and tail, and then add a series of short, curved lines along the underside of the body for the armored scales. Finally, add some circles around the body for the underwater bubbles. Keep the bubbles clustered together in small groups.

10

Erase any guide lines you no longer need and re-draw any final sketch lines that you'd like to fix.

MAKE IT DIFFERENT
Dragons are mythical creatures, so you can change them however you want! You can re-create these drawings as best you can, or you can use your creativity to make them different. Give a dragon bigger horns or wings, add a pattern, or color them in. If you colored in this dragon, what colors would you choose? What other underwater elements could you incorporate into this drawing?

Because this dragon is underwater, the light source is at the top, so add shadows accordingly. Then use a dark value for the horns, spikes, and tail fin. Add medium value on the body and slightly darker value for spots. The underside of the body, inner ear, jaw, and webbing should be lighter, and the eye the lightest so it stands out.

WIND DRAGON

1

Start with three circles as guides for the body and head. Pay attention to the size and spacing between the circles. The farther apart you place the circles, the longer the body will be. Leave enough space on the left for the long tail.

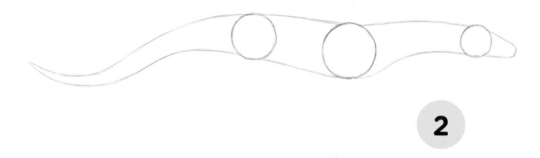

2

Connect the circles to form the neck and body. Add a muzzle on the right and a long tail on the left. The thin, sleek, snake-like body is what makes this a wind dragon.

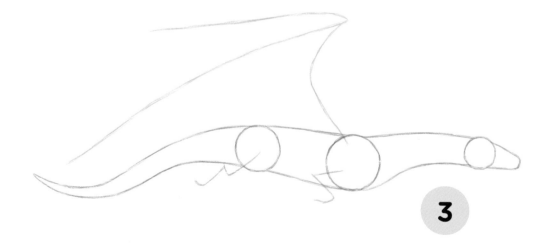

3

Add a guide for the wing, as well as two leg guides. Note where the guides curve and bend.

4

To draw the first part of the head, add piercing eyes and two spiky brow ridges. Add the sleek, beak-like muzzle, including a bump for the nostril. Angle the line to the left to create the mouth.

5

Complete the bottom jaw, add the other nostril, and then add two large, curvy horns on the back of the head, as well as one additional cone-shaped horn above the jaw.

Following the guide, draw the first part of the wing, making the base thicker and adding a curved spike at the top. Then add the tucked-in front leg. Use short, curved lines to emphasize the muscle structure at the top, and at the bottom, draw a couple of small, pointy shapes for the digits.

6

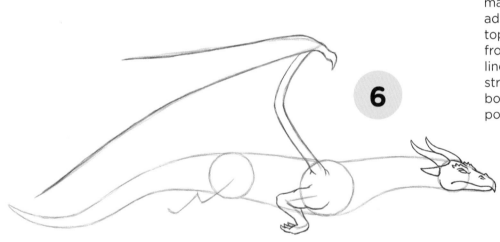

Finish the wing with a few straight and curved lines. Then add the hind leg in a similar way as the first leg.

7

8

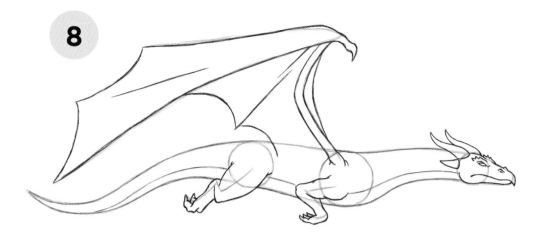

Use the remaining guides to draw the rest of the body. Draw a line along the lower edge of the body for the separation of the top and the underside. Don't overlap the shape of the wing or legs as you make these lines.

9

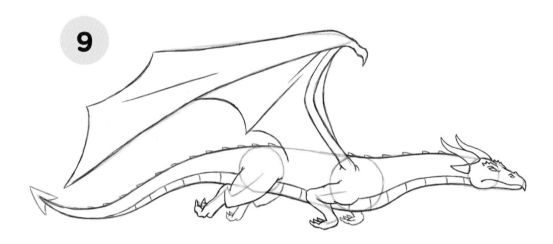

Using the first legs as templates, draw the visible portions of the other two. Then add short, vertical lines across the bottom of the body for scales, small spikes on the back, and an arrow-like spike on the tip of the tail.

10

Use the first wing as a template to draw the visible parts of the other wing.

11

Clean up your drawing to get it ready for shading!

12

First add shadows where they should appear on the body if the light source is coming from above. Add a medium value to the tops of the wings and body. A dark value helps give structure to the tops of the wings. Also add a dark value to the horns, spikes, around the eye, and on the claws. Leave the undersides a light value and the eye white. Add some stripes in the body and squiggly lines in the wings for texture.

CHINESE DRAGON

Draw three circles for the head and body.

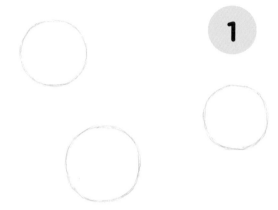

Draw two lines in the head, which are construction lines that will help you place the facial features. Then connect the head and body, and add a tail on the right.

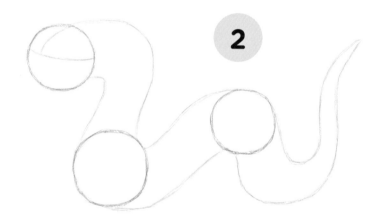

Draw guides for the muzzle, as well as for the four legs and feet.

GUIDE LINES Remember to sketch in guide lines lightly, and don't worry if your circles aren't perfect. You will erase guide lines later on, so instead of worrying about making a perfect circle, focus more on its size and placement in relation to the rest of the shapes.

4

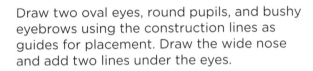

Draw two oval eyes, round pupils, and bushy eyebrows using the construction lines as guides for placement. Draw the wide nose and add two lines under the eyes.

5

Draw the mouth and teeth, and include a mustache made of wavy V shapes. Then draw two long whiskers coming off of the face from either side of the nose.

6

Finish the mouth, including the tongue. Then add the bushy bottom jaw, an ear, and the top of the head.

7

Draw an antler on the head, and then add the voluminous mane with wavy V shapes of different sizes. To complete the head, add the visible portion of the other antler.

Use the guide lines to draw the legs that are on this side of the body. The feet have three toes in front and one in the back. Add a claw at the tip of each toe. On the top-left side of the hind leg, draw flame-like fur using a series of wavy lines. Add a smaller bit of this fur to the back of the leg too.

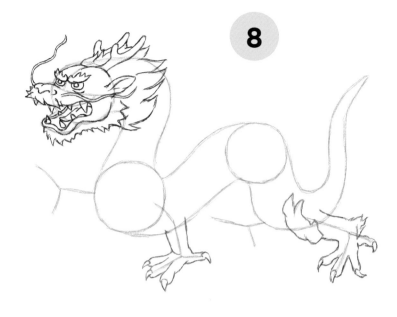

Complete the guide for the body, without overlapping the legs, and add some triangle shapes to the tip of the tail. Add the two other legs, including a small tuft of fur on the back of the front leg.

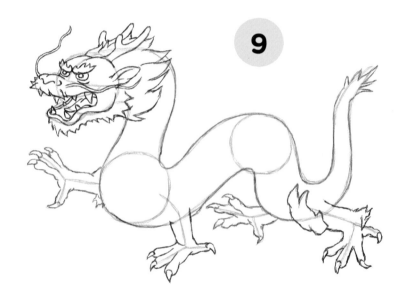

Draw spikes along the back. At the end of the tail, make the tip similar to a flame. Add flame-like fur to the front leg, as well.

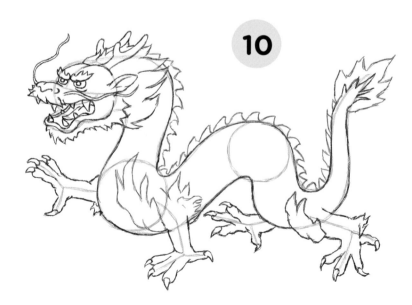

For more graphic illustration, try inking your drawing. Carefully go over the final sketch lines with a pen, marker, or any other type of permanent ink. After inking, remove the pencil marks with an eraser for a cleaner drawing.

Don't worry about shading this dragon to make it look three-dimensional. If you have colored pencils or markers, you can color it any way you'd like! For a pencil drawing, use a light value on the mane, mustache, beard, antlers, spikes, tip of tail, and underside. Leave the eyes, whiskers, and claws white. The darkest value is in the mouth and just above the eyes, and a middle-to-dark value is prominent on the rest of the body, with darker marks for scales. Leave a lighter area running along the middle of the body for a highlight.

FLYING DRAGON

1

Lightly sketch three circles as guides for the head and body.

2

Add a muzzle and a tail. Then connect the head and body circles.

3

Add two long lines with a bend in the middle to create the guides for the wings. Then add leg guides with lines that bend where the joints will be.

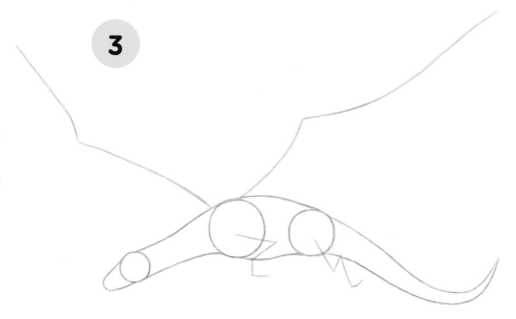

4

Start with the eye shape, leaving it blank inside. Draw the spiky brow above and a hint of the brow on the other side of the head. Add the pointy, beak-like muzzle, two nostrils, and teeth.

5

Finish the bottom jaw with a wavy line and add two horns coming from the jaw. Add small triangular spikes down the middle and a large, curvy horn on either side of the head.

6

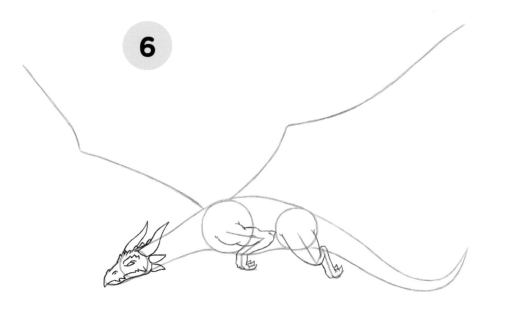

Draw the two tucked-in legs on this side of the body using the guides below the body. Use curved lines to emphasize the muscle structure and add pointy digits that face backward.

7

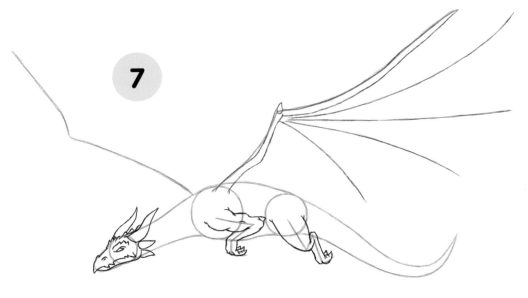

Start the first wing by making the guide line thicker and adding a spike. Then add four additional lines for the bones that make up the inside structure of the wing.

Complete the first wing by making the bones thicker, and then connect the tips with curved lines. Start on the second wing. Follow the guide line and add a spike, and use a dashed line to suggest this bone in the wing.

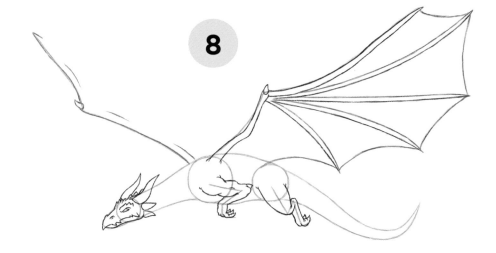

Again use broken lines to suggest the bones in the second wing. Connect the tips with curved lines. Then use the remaining guides to draw the rest of the body. Draw a line along the lower edge of the body. Make sure not to overlap the wing or legs as you darken the lines.

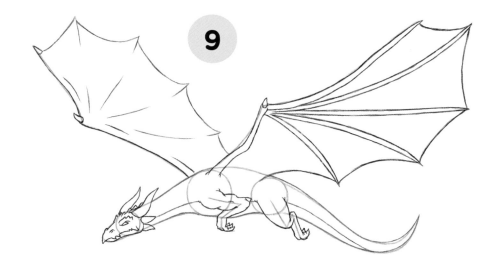

Draw the visible portions of the other two legs the same way you drew the first. Then draw a series of short, vertical lines across the bottom of the body for the scales. Draw small spikes on the back and an arrow-like shape for a spike on the tip of the tail.

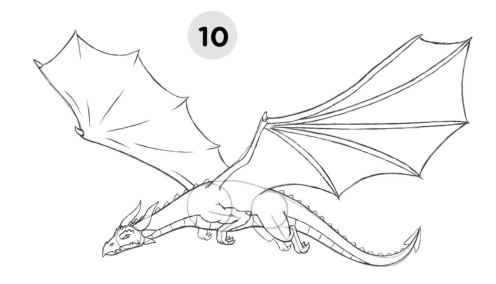

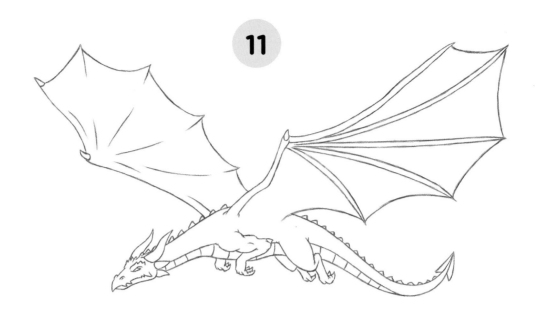

For a cleaner look, erase as much as you can of the initial guide lines. Don't worry about erasing all of them. It's okay to leave some behind. Also re-draw any final sketch lines that you may have accidentally erased.

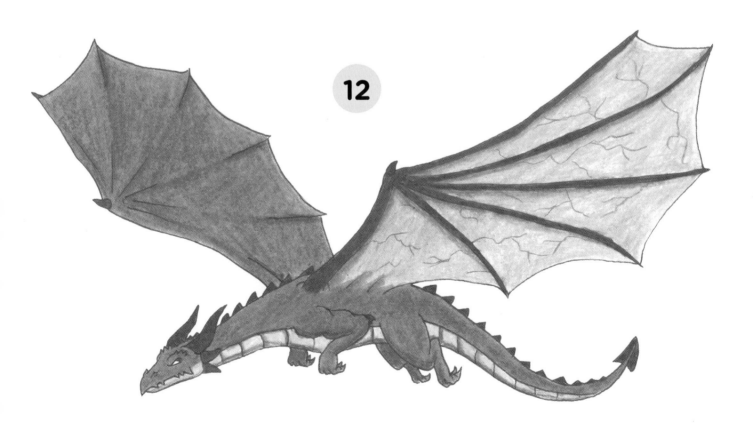

Add some shadows to make your drawing look more three-dimensional. For this look, use a dark value on the spikes, horns, and bones in the wings. Use a medium value on most on most of the body, but the scales on the underside of the body and the inside of the wing should be a light value. Add some squiggly lines on the wing for veins.

ABOUT THE AUTHOR

How2DrawAnimals.com teaches beginning artists how to draw all kinds of animals from A to Z through video demonstrations and simple step-by-step instructions. Started in 2012 by an animal-loving artist with a bachelor's degree in illustration, How2DrawAnimals offers a new tutorial each week and now boasts hundreds of animal drawing tutorials. Working in graphite and in colored pencils, and in both realistic and cartoon styles, How2DrawAnimals has featured animals from all letters of the alphabet, from Aardvark to Zebra and everything in between. See more at How2DrawAnimals.com.

ALSO IN THE LET'S DRAW SERIES:

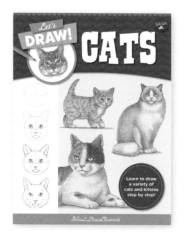

Let's Draw Cats
ISBN: 978-0-7603-8070-3

Let's Draw Dogs
ISBN: 978-0-7603-8072-7

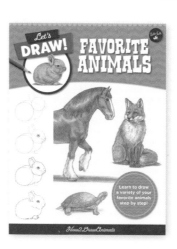

Let's Draw Favorite Animals
ISBN: 978-0-7603-8074-1

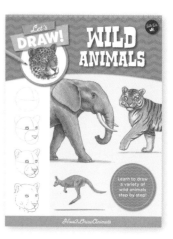

Let's Draw Wild Animals
ISBN: 978-0-7603-8076-5

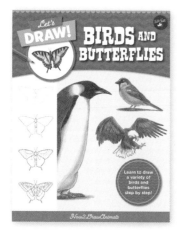

Let's Draw Birds & Butterflies
ISBN: 978-0-7603-8078-9

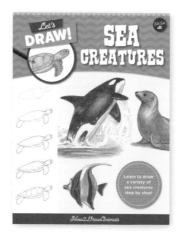

Let's Draw Sea Creatures
ISBN: 978-0-7603-8080-2

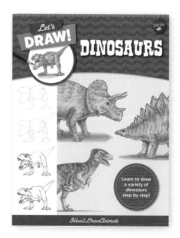

Let's Draw Dinosaurs
ISBN: 978-0-7603-8082-6

Inspiring | Educating | Creating | Entertaining

www.WalterFoster.com